From Jon

The Tiger

This book has been reviewed
for critical accuracy by

Carroll R. Norden, Ph.D.
Professor of Zoology
University of Wisconsin — Milwaukee

Copyright © 1993 Steck-Vaughn Company
Copyright © 1979, Raintree Publishers Limited Partnership

All rights reserved. No part of the material protected by this copyright may be reproduced or utilized in any form by any means, electronic or mechanical, including photocopying, recording, or by any information storage and retrieval system, without permission in writing from the copyright owner. Requests for permission to make copies of any part of the work should be mailed to: Copyright Permissions, Steck-Vaughn Company, P.O. Box 26015, Austin, TX 78755. Printed in the United States of America.

Library of Congress Number: 79-13604

5 6 7 8 9 10 11 12 13 14 15 16 17 W 99 98 97 96 95 94 93

Printed in the United States of America.

Library of Congress Cataloging in Publication Data

Hogan, Paula Z
  The tiger.

  Cover title: The life cycle of the tiger.
  SUMMARY: Describes in simple terms the life cycle of tigers.
  1. Tigers—Juvenile literature. [1. Tigers]
I. Mikec, Larry. II. Title. III. Title: The
life cycle of the tiger.
QL737.C23H63 599'.74428 79-13604
ISBN 0-8172-1506-9 hardcover library binding
ISBN 0-8114-6438-5 softcover library binding

The
TIGER

By Paula Z. Hogan
Illustrations by Larry Mikec

RAINTREE
STECK-VAUGHN
PUBLISHERS
The Steck-Vaughn Company

Austin, Texas

Tigers live in the jungle. They hunt alone.

A tiger's orange fur is the color of dry grass. Its black stripes look like shadows. In their forest home, tigers are hard to see unless they are very close.

Tigers rest when the sun beats down. Their soft footpads cannot touch hot ground. Night must fall before they hunt.

Soft footpads allow tigers to hunt without a sound. They listen for animals moving through the forest.

Night after night animals come to the water hole. The tiger hides near the path. As an animal passes, the tiger jumps at its neck.

To get enough meat, tigers must hunt large animals. Often they kill the young or the sick. A full-grown animal could fight back.

After tiger cubs are born, their mother keeps them clean by licking them. Baby tigers are blind and helpless. Their eyes open after a few days.

After three months the cubs see well enough to follow their mother. A female raises her cubs alone.

Cubs wait in tall grass. When it grows dark their mother brings meat. She lets her babies eat first.

Young tigers learn to hunt by watching their mother. Later she looks on while the cubs kill small animals.

Of all cats, only tigers swim. The mother stands in the water. She calls to her young with a soft purr.

After one year of age, males leave their mothers. Females leave eight months later. The young tigers find hunting grounds of their own.

Every year tigers are shot and skinned. Their skins make beautiful coats. If this goes on, all the wild tigers will be gone.

Tigers, leopards, lions, and pumas are big cats. Lions stay in family groups. But most cats live alone like the tiger.

GLOSSARY

These words are explained the way they are used in this book. Words of more than one syllable are in parentheses. The heavy type shows which syllable is stressed.

cub — a baby tiger
footpad (**foot**·pad) — the bottom part of an animal's foot.
forest (**for**·est) — trees and plants that cover a large area of land.
full-grown — having grown up to become an adult
fur — the thick, hairy coat of an animal
helpless (**help**·less) — not able to take care of itself
hunting grounds (**hunt**·ing grounds) — areas where tigers find meat
jungle (**jun**·gle) — a hot, rainy forest
leopard (**leop**·ard) — a large, strong cat that has spotted fur
lion (**li**·on) — a large, strong cat that lives in family groups
puma (**pu**·ma) — a large cat, also called cougar or mountain lion
purr — a soft sound that cats make
shadows (**shad**·ows) — dark areas
skinned — having the skin cut off
water hole (**wa**·ter hole) — a small pond